MW00581396

BY ANDREW SCHELLING

Old Growth: Selected Poems & Notebooks 1986-1994

The India Book

Tea Shack Interior

Wild Form, Savage Grammar

Two Elk: A High Country Notebook

Old Tale Road

From the Arapaho Songbook

A Possible Bag

The Real People of Wind & Rain

Tracks Along the Left Coast:
Jaime de Angulo & Pacific Coast Culture

EDITING

The Wisdom Anthology of North American Buddhist Poetry

Love and the Turning Seasons:
India's Poetry of Spiritual & Erotic Longing

TRANSLATION

Dropping the Bow: Poems of Ancient India

The Cane Groves of Narmada River

Songs of the Sons & Daughters of Buddha
(with Anne Waldman)

Erotic Love Poems from India

Bright as an Autumn Moon: Fifty Poems from the Sanskrit

Some Unquenchable Desire:
Sanskrit Poems of the Buddhist Poet Bhartrihari

THE FACTS AT
DOG TANK
SPRING

ANDREW SCHELLING

DOS MADRES

2020

DOS MADRES PRESS INC.
P.O. Box 294, Loveland, Ohio 45140
www.dosmadres.com   editor@dosmadres.com

Dos Madres is dedicated to the belief that the small press is essential
to the vitality of contemporary literature as a carrier of the new voice,
as well as the older, sometimes forgotten voices of the past. And in an
ever more virtual world, to the creation of fine books pleasing to the
eye and hand.

Dos Madres is named in honor of Vera Murphy and Libbie Hughes,
the "Dos Madres" whose contributions have made this press possible.

Dos Madres Press, Inc. is an Ohio Not For Profit Corporation and a
501 (c) (3) qualified public charity. Contributions are tax deductible.

Executive Editor: Robert J. Murphy

Illustration & Book Design: Elizabeth H. Murphy
www.illusionstudios.net

Typeset in Adobe Garamond Pro, Quinquefoliolate & Spirals
ISBN 978-1-953252-04-3
Library of Congress Control Number: 2020945480

First Edition

ACKNOWLEDGMENTS:

ANTHOLOGIES—*Cascadian Zen: Bioregional Writings on Cascadia Here and Now* (Paul E Nelson, Jason M. Wirth), *Counter Desecration: A Glossary of Writing for the Anthropocene* (Linda Russo, Marthe Reed), *The End of the World Anthology* (Richard Lopez, John Bloomberg-Rissman, T.C. Marshall), *Poetics for the More-Than-Human-World* (Mary Newell, Sarah Nolan, Bernard Quetchenbach)

PERIODICALS—*Catamaran, Dispatches from the Poetry Wars, The Emerald Tablet, Kritya* (India), *Longhouse, Poetry Flash, Seedings*

CHAPBOOKS—Longhouse, Woodland Pattern

BROADSIDE—Smokeproof Press (Brad O'Sullivan)

Luggage tag poem (Elizabeth Robinson)

RESIDENCY—Woodland Pattern Book Center at the Lynden Sculpture Garden, Milwaukee, May 2015

Thanks to the Denver Art Museum (Jaime Kopke) for commissioning "Mount Blanca with Ute Creek at Dawn"

Author Photograph, Andrea Becker

To the Memory of Dale Pendell

1947-2018

People change their gods and their mythologies
more readily and quickly than they change
their declensions and conjugations, and more
capriciously. Rules can be formulated to predict
how a given Indo-European phoneme will turn
out in Old High German or Pale Dry Tocharian,
but the mutations of divinities or of mythical
motifs are subject to no rules.
    Martin L. West,
    Indo-European Poetry and Myth

Clefs, chirps, upward glides, falling whistles
    Susan Howe, *Concordance*

TABLE OF CONTENTS

I.

TENTH SONG OF THE MEADOWLARK

II.
MOUNT BLANCA
WITH UTE CREEK AT DAWN

III.
MISCELLANIES, INVENTIONS, & FINDS

IV.
RIDDLERS, ROGUES, & CHILDREN

I

TENTH SONG
OF THE
MEADOWLARK

LONG TAIL

        Picture the distant place
ice & rock, high above
                inkcolored pines

a pungent odor lingers by the backdoor

where power concentrates
Arapaho, *neséíhi*
wild, untamed, a twitch of

            whiskers the quick

precise whip of the weasel tail

there are no gods to appease

        just chainsaws, far off
snap of target practice
          darting in & out of a ground squirrel
             burrow

        I'll put on a jacket & tie
walk the streets at night

pubs full of colorful people

THE HERMENEUTICAL TASK

When the sign says don't go past this sign you know
something's up there. Stick figure with horns, mountain
sheep floating on rock face, spirals catch the slow rotation
of stars, if you sit & watch long enough. Each cairn wavers
in sunlight its sentinel lizard a flash of blue. I think the two
kestrel CB spotted chasing the raven into vertically slashed
shadow WE DON'T HAVE ENOUGH WILDERNESS.
There's no way to figure why this slab got so many spindly
serpents or NIGHT SKY INITIATIVE rivers. Land is alive
here LIZARD LIZARD blue throat the lonesome song of
the canyon wren.

> In an oral tradition
> the only way to achieve
> the hermeneutical task of understanding a
> story is
>
> "to perform it"

Chaco Canyon vi:2014

THIRD PARTY MOUNTAIN DOG

Not hunter-gather shamans
but scavenge-monger
constructivists

says J.B. Bryan when he ferrets through
                    the archaic

            Kinnikinnik tea would
        be something else
                pocket gopher infusion
                        trim coyote bacon paw
I woke up missing my love

O ancient western lineage your red pot designs
so like that woman
            she folds into a plié

out at the edge of Chaco
            bent juniper baked clay

3

TOLOACHE

for Jennifer

Gypsy flower
        psychotrope
fall in love, they say toloache
good for alcohol sickness
        good for seeing the future
someone gives you the toloache flower—
white trumpet-vine
        fence climber purple veins

When will Fleche Amarillo deliver my missing
equipage? my notebooks?
spare clothes?

I'll give it a try
toloache
        but they say datura can kill
        you

Pátzcuaro, 31 October 2001

4

THIRTEEN NOTEBOOKS

Thirteen notebooks have passed
since I worked at this poem
a friend with ice blue eyes once called the
poem
an archetype
what did he mean?
Many tracks twist
through its chirps & clefts
that's one thought
It has portals and by-ways another
Now Jack Collom has gone straight through—
out west you still hear talk of the
land of the dead
gullies & animal tracks
The next life's not certain Jack
you are now on your own
compadré

2 July 2017

BACK IN THE HILLS

Back in the hills the gambling goes on
    cebiihínee
          fists closing
    around four deer leg dice

        two bonelengths scored by a
rawhide knot

My brother sent foreleg shafts
UPS from where the buck went down
—still tight with fur
I boiled off the sinew
a hack saw, then ground the ends smooth
on a rock
        Paleo north Asiatic variant
songs coming from under the hill

    from so far-off, such queer lyrics
    nobody quite remembers the meaning
        "a blackbird
          I track you wherever"

might be a puberty song

Water follows its underground cycle
    there goes a whisk of raven wing

    high on the talus a burnt-out bristlecone

    black stones in a ring

ARROYO

We crisscross the southwest by car,
shadows, aridity, broken moments
      of pasture

—laugh when the car turns past a green
swathe

of hair,
wild mustangs
lower, hungry to find who you are,
back of rough pleasure   crinkled, dark
Canyon of the Ancients
    a nib of moisture slips down the rimrock—

      I wrote you a poem about piñon jays
      heart's a feathered thing there,
         you carried the pulse of it

   We slept and overnight the kiva turned to rubble

Some poems didn't get written
some bones frighten everyone
     they wash down the arroyo
    they shiver   even

    your forearms shiver

TENTH SONG OF THE MEADOWLARK

The tenth song of the meadowlark
a user's manual
for the bioregion
This watershed moves like a raga
it begins, as birds, slowly waken at dawn
scattered here-and-there notes
crescendo into a chaos, all songs all at once
Some passerines learn the wrong melody
imitation is often imperfect
Tilt your head to hear more distinctly
sleep loo lidi lidijuvi
       or do you hear *sleep loo lidi lidijivu*
The western male meadowlark, his yellow
vest his black v-shaped collar
Ornithologists now recognize nine songs
The tenth I use to make
      medicine

THAT BLACK BIB

That black bib that yellow
breast that tattoo
          a five-point star from years in the Air Force
I'd take that if I could
to remember you
you carried it always? even as it fades?
Protection yes, but from what
do you need protection
could you have held it to barter
in the afterlife, Jack—?
Nepalese women once kept their ankle tattoos
          swapping for food in the Newar bardo
I'll swap you a sandwich then beat
our chevron wings up fourth
of july valley
past the historic mine past the glacier
We come from similar cultures
we still reincarnate
as birds

SHE TALKED ABOUT SPEARHEADS

She talked about spearheads
at Caribou Lake they had
no notches
that's the Folsom style
wood sinew leather
many plant fibers if you know
how to harvest them
Meanwhile quiver might go back to a Mongol
word
Beads do you know
how hard it is to make a bead?
have you ever tried to make a bead?
There is a white bed
of clay
you will not ever
find it you wrote a poem near it once
you used the word
communist
a word that's fallen into disuse
Canyon of the Ancients
tucked into the corner where there is
no map

for Jane Wodening

ONE QUESTION

One question
where does a book begin
does it begin the last 1000 years
paper, parchment
sheep's hide, palm-leaf, bamboo
it changes what you think of the pictograph
to see frog as a clan sign
horned figure pecked into
desert varnish
it was cold the night Jack Collom died
we had a dream
we were chipping acrostics
into Precambrian rock

IN HIS VISIONS

In his visions he's
composing acrostics
the dying enter a sphere of visions
this one's a no shooting zone
the binding is Japanese, externally sewn,
he inscribes it for me in running grass script
black ink jotting left to right
scent of ozone in the atmosphere
grief preys on the living but
not the dead I hear
Footfall darjeeling flute-blade sunlight day
can you give your name away?
that's from a friend
a poet whose name I withhold
We all might have been going to have lived
a long, long time in the future
on this continent shaped by geologic force
outlaws & anarchists by the fire.
Kishori Amonkar, can you hear her sing
the rain-season song
she regulates the monsoon
the Southern Rockies washed by thunder
skirts of rain
trailing down valley
Can some riddler out there answer me?
why is love so difficult?

SHELF SUPPORT

Shelf support is of wood
there's an old splintered board
for backing
Bodhisattva image or Catholic Saint
Saturday we did the firing
my various cups had varying success
two blew to smithereens
a single firing of one exquisite pot
the people here make replicas not facsimiles
digging sheep dung
from a hundred year old Navajo corral
to get a Hopi blush
it's an off-gassing masterpiece
the next kiln will be at Blanding
a white clay vein at Edge of the Cedars
piñon jays guard it
Sleeping Ute Mountain casts
its shadow from
the south

HIS HEART GOES TO THE NORTH

His heart goes to the north
people move about
like flocks of birds there
none of that ritual tightness, none of that
priests acting important
         so many places they do that

Nomad is the California style
One comrade from the Left Coast writes
"shy of my small breasts...
other times fearless, a warrior...
my spear-tip nipples"

What could I do but pick sage near Tres Piedras
while the wind blew
ghost train tracks running past
I see the cabin Aldo Leopold built
we have yet to evolve a community that honors the land
wood & sinew for a hunter's bow
         a crescent moon

Once a commune thrived, here in the piñon woods
They called it Drop City

A CHEREMISS SONG

for Anselm Hollo, 1934-2013

Anselm has gone now
dropped into the valley, followed
      the whitewater stream

kestrel circles & dips over meadow

      What remains are words of his
Cheremiss song, *I shouldn't have started
these red wool mittens,*
my sister in law pinned them up
over her loom
kept them for decades

Like caribou he came from the taiga
taught me a lot about translating poetry
                —just use this
horn-handled knife
these birch-wood song sticks
a bit of theory helps now & then

Mittens & poems they're done now,
you go ahead, Anselm
take good care
those fjord-croaking ravens will greet you—
Your poems hold a cheer
no one else managed

      the mittens lasted a lifetime.

I shouldn't have started these red wool mittens.
they're done now,
but my life is over.

STALIN WAS SKEPTICAL

Stalin was skeptical
chamber music
did not advance his gigantic plan
a string quartet might get you murdered
If Anselm were here there'd be someone
to recount the 20th century's history
Fifty or more
magpies drop into
the boughs of two fir
boisterous agitated several
sail off
The blue sky the loud rusty call
I wonder if there's a code
to decipher this oldest bog Latin
      whole hillside pitching with cries
      filled with strident winged creatures
Remember the hobo camp
back of Depot Square?
before the yellow bulldozers came
a parking lot for Savings & Loan,
it sounded
like that.

THE HAND THAT SHAPES THE MIND

The hand that shapes the mind
clay or written word
is subject to accident & time
to find it you must find the meander
they say things too pure or
lines that go straight
permit troublesome spirits a place to cling
The good teacup has a flaw
it wobbles
The avant-garde continues with its own purity
an exotic not very hardy species,
survives in greenhouse environments
academia the so-called
art world
the gallery ghettos
once set outside it tends to shrivel and die
who can maintain that level of purity?
On the phone a message
how many years old
I intend to keep it my dead father's voice
it may help me imagine a new Kuksu
a place in the future the watershed no longer
imperiled
a bird mask to cover
I like to think sheepishly disclose
a lifetime of error
one accidental imprint in the design
a crack in the pot
where the spirit escapes

PERCUSSION BONE NARRATOR

Not identified yet, says the paper
a species of humans hanging out
at the Cerutti Mastodon site
massive bones found during highway construction
outside San Diego
          true, this pushes inhabitance
back 100,000 years.

Hammer & anvil
bone percussion technology
the pegmatite cobbles
the andesite fractures change what a human once was
now North America hangs,
a drop of dew on a squaw-berry leaf.

How will I ever leave this old world
bronze aspen leaves rattling over the
Middle Fork
ice cold October ripples?
friends, daughter, lover, books all gone into
a realm of might be.

Bone & molar percussion get at my entrails
a negative flake scar knife
dividing the sinew?
The cow moose who gave that *get the fuck
out of here* snort,
when I climbed into Wheeler Basin?

In *Nature* the article says at the

Cerutti site is no sign
of butchery, could or would be,
the subjunctive mode that always sent a sharp
chill down my groin.

Its "ancient, cloudy, moody powers,"
Ursula K. Le Guin writes of the grammatical mode
regretting its disuse today.
A world of would, could, should, might, may—
Who might hammer these bones
for marrow?
Who cooked up the outlandish belief in rebirth, the could,
the wobbling should of it—
what might those ancients envision?
How far back would we go?

I ALWAYS HOPED TO WRITE YOU A SONG

I always hoped to write you a song
sad little cracked tune
other birds fly off the magpies get raucous
trash birds you call them
song with no beginning
You never had no beginning neither
so many objects crack
The refrain changes, words fall into disuse
one note showed up in the Perseid
medicine belt
meteors all over Sugarloaf
wild oregano's purple thistle
that whapping string of prayer flags on the
northwest ridge
You drop your clothes on the tiles
ballet shoes down the stairs
they lie there
twisted
like four clocks
set to different times.

YES, BUT HOW

Yes, but how
does raga recharge
the seasons, catchments & drainages, the watches of
day & night, the *prahars*?
Why Todi at daybreak
Malkauns at midnight?
Terry Riley said he would
pass along insights
gotten from Pandit Pran Nath years ago
Vidya Rao told me
she'd hold onto the question *how*
Then a comrade I'd met in college
told the story of lessons in Oakland—
telephone cables or electric lines passed the window
When Pran Nath sang
sparrows & warblers perched
motionless facing the room
When my friend took the tamboura
off they flew.

WHY I VISIT THE CAMEL FESTIVAL

One neighbor, against
expectation
keeps a Bactrian camel in a corral   two shaggy
dark humps—
     with a Palomino

I'd like to visit the Mongolia camel festival
it's got soldiers, monks, merchants,
camel breeders   but instead

     go to the Associated Writing Programs.
The camel fair has races, music, dance,
women & men show up in costume
and compete for attention
—which sounds like the AWP

Turn anywhere, there's stamping & snorting
wheels, grunts,
merchants haul in their loads
     they hand out books, brochures, buttons with
tough gnomic verse

People have traveled from Louisiana
Oklahoma   Oregon   far-off Singapore
New York

in the convention hall
water's scarce   hardly any vegetation
just like the Asiatic steppes

The tribes stamp noisily here,
           they snort with impatience
hoofs clop in the corridors
imagine your fingers tangled in camel hair,
           it smells smoky & fierce

Minneapolis Convention Center, April 2015

24

THEY SHOW UP MAGICAL, SCARY

"Hairy, downy, pileated"
writes a friend, of local bird life

here we watch mostly
          the gang of eight
(bucks on the mountain above)

the birds that winter over
are magpie

          all else but a few hawks
          gone down slope with the snow

less wind thicker trees

Althea and Chas saw a black fox
maybe the one I met
          last summer

in headlights
remote bit of road in the gulch

a small population in Colorado
the book says they show up magical, scary in
Celtic lore

          none survive
on the British Isles

AN ARAPAHO VERB

An Arapaho verb *neséíhi*
to be wild
       it is animate & intransitive
for those who like grammar.
There go four early morning doe
       thin hooves on autumn colored grasses
verbs for animate or inanimate things
it's a cosmology
like Indo-European
makes words male female neuter
Neséíhi's animate
act spontaneous, travel far, take risks, be alone,
live where nature edges in
you don't let nobody mess with you
you stay skeptical of things
Not careless though—
let's sharpen & oil the tools, watch
our comrades, tell stories
cover a friend's belly & breasts with arnica oil
Then there's *níitóuuhu*
also animate—
we make wild animal noises
whimper, cry, sometimes go whistling
it's speech
the deer understand

THE MIMBRES KILL THEIR POTS

Place the black & white earthenware over your dead
cover her face
bust a hole
in the base to depart from—

      it is over

      that's all there is to it

You are stuffed
in a clay pot tied off with skin

dropped in a crevice
blown by a thousand year wind

          canis major

                corona borealis

      andromeda   flicker & vanish

No longer a daylight person
you won't phone your children one by one
Sunday *Times* on your lap
or take coffee and crackers for lunch

you see things now we who
remain only guess at

Great Star path
overhead

for Corinne Schelling
1924-2011

ENDING WITH A LINE BY ELSA CROSS

Poets of old
        Greece & Rome
    took out their rivals with
    tiny lethal epigrams
masters of sarcasm, the clever put-down.
In Michoacán
the *calavera*, fortune cookie death inscription
        the tiny poem goes to your friend
        sugar skull carries her name
            what do you write for her
tombstone?

I'll miss you los Muertos
miss you la Catrina, la Flaca, la Huesuda, la Pelona
you have given us
            new tastes for poetry

fancy skinny bony bald
we like to make love buck naked, we like our
poems not dressed up

Village mantled in pine smoke
volcanic peaks,
        vague clouds.

Día de los Muertos

ULA

Thick darkness
drinks
the last glint of sunlight.
Crows quit raiding the temple food,
no more *caww caww*
heading back to high roosts.
An owl tests the night cautiously
presses its beak through a tree-hole
neck sunk in feathers
head squat as a
   hand drum.

       Viddūka
       from *Vidyākara's Sanskrit anthology*

Crow and owl are primordial enemies. One
inhabits the day the other the night. A fledgling
crow, never seen an owl, will raise the alarm
at a glimpse. In Massachusetts a birdwatcher
photographed a barn owl kill a crow and fifty
crows retaliate. Viddūka's poem catches primordial
enmity. READ JACK COLLOM'S POETRY
too. Owl comes through Old High German, *ula*.
Behind the word is a verb, to turn, turn around,
as the owl's head. One Sanskrit term for crow is
ulūkajit, defeater of owls.

   for Kwang Mae Cho

SOLSTICE WATCHER

Happy birthday Terry Riley may the music
continue
here comes
daddy coyote with jackrabbit
conejo
clenched in his jawbone beware,
the word has a vulgar meaning as well

     & the Albuquerque clan
     transmutes
     national park campsite Chaco Canyon
     into

       "home"

     Dutch oven enchiladas
     Mike hollers over poetry while
     Cirrelda and Cherrymae retreat to the tents
     oh hornéd figure
     rock cut sunburst Wijiji is

a solstice watcher?

Pass the winebottle   red rimrock shade

Peter Garland says the bioregion needs a few
empty beer cans
this poem's for him
Oh to visit Southern Ute spring season
                    Bear Dance again
rock dagger sunlight
wild west megafauna

24 June 2014

THE DEER A PIECE OF OLD RAWHIDE

The deer a piece of old rawhide
north a mudslide took out the Pfeifer bridge
a mountain came down
at Mud Creek
look how active:
                        crow   crow   crow
Walking the empty coast highway
down to Nepenthe
I want you here holding my hand
you are here
maybe better you didn't come
            crow   crow
                        crow   crow
The past is angular it's
watching some future disaster
jays redwoods bay-laurel
skin water blouse thighs tears
your tears my voice dry as the tough oak-leaf
tanbark oak at Bixby's landing
thigh next to thigh
one more
time

EARLY

Early to wake
a horned owl blows a pale white hole
through the woods
heading
down canyon towards town
the dark bed, the dark forest,
        you have your karma as well

AFTER CLIMBING MOUNT YALE

Grease snapping
over the twigs
fingers black turning the meat
We're down from the
high country
down from the quick July snow squall
tough backstrap of venison over the coals.
Eagles up there
down here a tangle of human plans
whiskey don't kill me
        I could live till I die.

A CONDOR BURIAL IN LARKSPUR

In Larkspur diggers turn up bones
of a condor
bones of 100 black & grizzly bear
scatter of sea otter bones
a California village that dates back to the Pyramids
tools musical instruments harpoon tips spears
bones of a cougar
The way we bury things, put bones in the ground,
dab paint on the condor's wing feathers
but in California
who remembers what the old ones thought?
Today is total solar eclipse
11:45 a.m. smoky & cool
Clark's nutcracker going west gives
a jagged *craaaawk*
small birds perch unalarmed in a fir
you can walk right up to them in the grey air
flutes bone-awls hairpins game pieces
What raga do you sing
when the sun goes into wintry eclipse?
"The holy shit raga!"
Day moves to dawn
        to dusk to dawn and back.

SONG

the sky is a dome
blue   azure   windblown   shell
a five foot bullsnake
in road dust
khaki with shoe-leather florets
people with a cell phone
come take photos
sky never not moving
blue   blue-white   a turtle's transparent
shell

11

MOUNT BLANCA
WITH UTE CREEK AT DAWN

MOUNT BLANCA WITH UTE CREEK AT DAWN

Colorado is the headwaters state, a land of rivers & peaks.

Ute Creek drains eastward. It reverses course and flows southwest, joining the Rio Grande drainage, and brings nutrients to the Tewa-speaking pueblos of New Mexico.

Where Mt. Blanca sits was Mexico until 1848.

In Chinese, "mountains & rivers" means landscape, territory, sometimes nation. In modern terms, it could be watershed, drainage, acequia, bioregion.

The meeting ground of Art and Geology, first quick glimpse of Ecology.

The map in Tony Hillerman's detective novels locates Mt. Blanca on the right-hand margin. The peak stands at the eastern limit of the Navajo cosmography. I have not heard that skinwalkers go past it.

This is Maynard Dixon, the modern master of Southwest form & light. This is his cubist three-panel screen with arroyos and cañados in dark heron blue; exposed sunlit ridges burnt orange.

We are looking over Ute Creek from east to west, dawn to nightfall. Out there lie the San Juans, Southern Ute, Navajo, Hopi. The state's last grizzly was killed out there.

Our American rivers & creeks have been dammed, dredged, diverted, channeled, paved, redirected, bridged, polluted, & lit on fire. We have fished them, boated them, written books on them, drowned in their rapids, thrown trash in them, and pissed in their waters. The artist Christo hopes to wrap one of them, the Arkansas, just north, near Salida.

Painters fix objects onto their canvases. I've seen bottle caps, stones, animal fur, shreds of newspaper, a paintbrush, a small skull. Painters scrawl messages on their work too. A blade of jealousy sheers through me. Writers put only words on the page.

Letting your mind or mouth wander regarding religious matters may prove dangerous. Showing off is also perilous, I mean about things you know, or your skill in mountains. The gods are always watching for bright flamboyant figures, to carry off.

We are standing in the Huerfano Valley, named for a large cinder cone that rises like a strict guardian where the highway enters. The *huerfano*, orphan—has greeted those who enter the valley for centuries.

Here is a photo of La Veta Pass.

In the dream, my grandmother Bertha had written *Yertle the Turtle*.

The Sangre de Cristo Mountains, with Blanca as a great snowcap presence, were for a time the home of *penitentes* who would flog themselves, carrying their Christ past adobe pueblos & cottonwoods.

Directly behind Mt. Lindsay a climbing formation, the Iron Nipple. It is said that Turtle first brought clay from the ocean floor, so the earth could be made.

Little Bear & Twin Peaks.

Stories in some cultures are inanimate. They cannot wander about on their own. It is we, the people, who carry them—through the years, across the territories. *The Lorax,* a goofy trickster, why does he smile from the tee shirts of the women who sell tickets at Cinemark Theater?

A dangerous path your family left you on—amid divorce, financial trouble, and alcoholism—may finally prove a place of refuge. Even a kindly road.

My computer does not recognize Yertle or Lorax. It tries to change and into Andrew.

Behind that southern ridge, restless, lifting & falling, are the Great Sand Dunes, endlessly shifting with sediment blown in from the west. They are popular with motorists. Sand Hill Cranes migrate through.

The buckskin fringe on my medicine bag stands for what I do not know, things I will never understand, various things, way too many to mention.

If you drive Rt. 17 past Mt. Blanca, you can visit an alligator farm, a memorial to an American soldier killed in Iraq, and a platform for Flying Saucer viewing. Down in Antonito you can visit Colorado's oldest church, and a fortress constructed of hubcaps, bottle caps, scrap metal, and soda cans, dedicated to a JESUS whose sacrament is marijuana. Alcohol is kills, says a hand-painted board.

One climbing route to the summit is called Little Bear.

Wood, wolf fur, paint, canvas, cord, tin.

The Bear Dance, held by the Southern Ute at Ignacio, may be the oldest dance in North America. Two hunters learnt it from a grizzly that danced with a tree. My love & I danced it as *moraches* growled in the cedar enclosure. Archaic ursine power lumbered across our lives.

Clans of timber wolf, grizzly, Colorado lynx, fisher, wolverine, and other top-of-the-food-chain mammals have not been seen wild in Colorado in decades. What animals and plants can you expect to disappear this year, or next?

A name that has borne you through difficult times is a source of power. It keeps you on a straight path. Now is the time to give it away. It could prove useful to others. Do not be stingy.

The east & west flanks of Mt. Blanca are art & ecology.

Where they meet is a dance ground for mountain sheep.

MISCELLANIES, INVENTIONS, & FINDS

WOLF ACROSTIC

Where I first saw the river's name, Apishapa, it was Young's book
        on wolves. Three Toes of the Apishapa, one heck
Of a critter. Lost part of a paw to a trap. After that managed to evade
        every snap, snare, bait, bounty hunter, or range rider for a decade.
Later I wondered,
        how do you say the river's name?
Fishpaw was the clue, the settlers called it that since the Ute term
        'mossy creek' sounded weird.

a-PISH-a-paw

ARAPAHO GHOST DANCE SONGS

My father
circles me through the spirit world
then a moose a moose
    stood at my side

Bright moon
riding home with fresh bison through shadows

Our father,
    heiso-noonin,
our father the whirlwind
He's put on the crow-feather
headdress

Back at the time of
the FIRST PEOPLE
it was turtle who gave us the earth,
    says my father

48

❦

Seven crows
flap over the dead meat

❦

Yellow I fly
          yellow I fly
prairie-rose twined in my hair
soaring upwards
Hei'ei'ei!

❦

Out there a lone
buffalo
with him I will make medicine

❦

Children
I've taken the morning cross for a feather
children look—
          says our father

The earth
crow lifted the earth
crow carried it to us
    a'hene'heni'a'a'
    a'he'yene'hene

Children
look what we've done
the whites have fallen desolate
they've gone crazy
    ahe' yuhe' yu

Crow is making a ford in the river
now it's done
on the near bank he gathers
        his children

UNWANTED

Instead of Christo's "Over the Arkansas"

In 1997 the artists Christo & Jeanne-Claude filed for
permits to sling 5.9 miles of "silvery luminous fabric" over
the Arkansas River where it drops through a steep cañon.
Slated for a 2010 installation the project was delayed by
environmental impact reports, protests, and litigation.
The hang site runs along Highway 50, narrow two-lane
road that twists beneath colored cliffs: burgundy, slate
blue, sienna, chocolate, sage green. Christo proposes
1200 steel cables (death to eagles) anchored by twice that
many concrete blocks (death to Bighorn sheep) placed
by helicopter alongside working ranches & occasional
pieces of vernacular art. Near Swissvale an upended canoe
is a shrine to 'fish that got away.' Bales of hay with worn
cowboy boots sticking comically out. Christo's project will
take cranes, bulldozers, helicopters, tour buses, emergency
vehicles, and draw a half-million viewers. He calls these
"gentle disturbances."

Open with elders of Southern Ute burning sage,
then prayers, drums, speeches, while U.S. agencies hand
        back to the tribe
various public lands.

Celebrate the founding of Cotopaxi in 1873 by Russian
Jews fleeing the Tsar—
bonfires and immigration smoke-signals
up river & down.

@

Fishermen to lead an all-faiths sunrise gathering the morning
the Caddis fly hatches.

@

Organize intertribal powwow & benefit sell-off of Christo
memorabilia, so tourists spend money
among folk that can use it.

@

Week long reading from Zebulon Pike's army report
for Historic Heritage types.

@

Ute singers & cowboy poets along both riverbanks. Banjos,
buffalo jerky, fry bread & cotton candy.

@

Chamber of Commerce groups
sponsor *corrido* music &
old-time dance in community plazas.

✸

Boy and Girl Scout jamborees to reaffirm
the Endangered Species Act, Clean River Act, Clean Air Act
and Migratory Bird Act.

✸

Confucian banner unfurled on cliffs near Salida
PEACE UNDER HEAVEN / LET RIVERS FLOW FREE

✸

Invite U.S. senators
for haiku workshop and Bighorn sheep viewing.

✸

Rattlesnake education courses for East Coast art lovers.

✸

File permits with BLM & State Forest Service
so Christo can wrap their regional headquarters
in luminous fabric.

*Historical note: Stymied for two decades by eco-activists and
skeptical public land workers, in 2016 Christo abandoned
plans for "Over the River." Part of a twenty-year-long public
resistance, the above was printed as a broadside by Brad*

O'Sullivan at Smokeproof Press—attributed to Anonymito—
and posted around Salida, upriver from the proposed site.

LE LYCANTHROPE

i startled him
at wood's edge
at dawn
a werewolf molting his skin

stretched then in foliage he slept
his face so twisted
i fled aghast

from the French of Jaime de Angulo

55

TREES OF THE JOHN MUIR WAY

Scottish

An apple branch, sometimes a single apple, was passport to the Celtic Otherworld.

You can still see, alongside our cairns & stone circles, a rowan, roddan, or mountain ash, its scarlet berries the food of the Tuatha dé Danaan.

One eats hazel nut to acquire the power of prophecy.

Witches ride the broom, the blackthorn, or the ragweed.

Of vaguer tradition, the Druidic cult of the yew.

North American

Soft wood of the Incense cedar is favored for pencils.

Resin distillers suffered a number of puzzling explosions, now known to be caused by combustible oils of the Jeffrey pine.

Named for Sequoyah, inventor of the Cherokee alphabet, the redwood was introduced to Scotland in 1853.

Fir, from Old Norse *fyri-*
            fyriskógr   fir-woods

John Muir in the Alhambra Valley
        trenching his apple orchards.
     he never did take to farming. didn't much
         like to write.

water drawn down from his beloved Sierra snowfields

   too far to see through the haze.

MACBETH'S CATALOGUE OF DOGGES

Hounds

      Greyhounds

    Mungrels   Spaniels

Curres

      Showges

Water-Rugs

      Demy-Wolves

 House-Keeper

      Hunter

SONG OF THE SAND LILY

In geography, as in ecology, every detail reflects the whole landscape. Let's use the sand lily, *leucocrinum*, for the whitebreasted goddess,

> Odysseus, take my *kredemnon*

and flung her bikini.

Shreds of deer-hide flutter from staffs and rock slabs on the tundra. Here's where the game drives of prehistoric October took place. But the real people of snow and thunder have gone underground. In this life, friendship being the keenest directive, I nose the car south on 285, a day's journey down the Arkansas, the Rio Grande, the wide muddy Chama. Blistered sagebrush edging the piñon. When I stop to piss there are coyote bones under the juniper.

Stars crackle over the Sandias. I pull into Placitas. JB left the key. The door opens to a rash of wood, rawhide, scrap metal, pumpkin, and scapulae—the percussion *arkestra* which brings detail to the unseen world. Ethnomusicology? At first glance it's the xylophone clackers. Then pebble-filled gourd shakers. A deer-hoof rattle of California design. By the drum set a tortoise shell waits. Waits for what? Clang of the Chevrolet hubcap gong? Scrape of the elk jaw jagstick? Then the faint tune of the sand lily returns—

> Buy her a shawl
> buy her a pipe

buy her a gong for the afterlife

white bones under juniper
swept fear of death
from me

buy her a gong for the
afterlife tree

for JB and Cirrelda

IV

RIDDLERS,
ROGUES, & CHILDREN

NAVAHO GRAMMAR

for Kristina Loften

The tawny parched landscapes of
San Jose
       the glaring jet wings

       stucco   white dry grasses
one more year of worrisome drought
from San Jacinto to Mt. Shasta

       In my pocket my former wife's driver's license
our daughter carries the ashes

We live in a contentious era
wars, they don't seem to end, or cruelty—
so she spent years fighting injustice to animals

on my lap
Gladys Reichhard's
      Navaho Grammar
the old syllables hard to read, what a tough language
      does it carry the speech of faraway gods?

Corn maidens, blue corn-pollen girls
      hers was a mind oddly precise at times
      even through alcohol
         those hard last years

63

Well, the airlines have their rules, package of cinders—
has to go under the seat.
you who were
a barelegged mother once
        on grassy slopes of the East Bay

IN MY TRADITION

In my tradition we don't tell
coyote stories,
James said in Cañoncito—
until the first hard frost.
I marveled as the three hard syllables
fell like three
raven feathers, no, like kernels
from a raven's unguarded beak
Next morning blue corn *atole*, crisp
ice on the windshield when I took
the sleeping bag out
to the car
A pinch of corn pollen
rubbed on the hands for the drive north
I came through Blackhawk
canyon blasted into a furious gorge
dynamite & heavy
equipment Clear Creek's seen it all
a thousand yards casino glass & cement
bigger than Mesa Verde
      crow   crow   crow
rip up a wild place for thrills   crow   crow
How different is walking?
what's it to you gambler dog-face?
If your heart don't know
that walking is different than gambling
no one can tell you
      crow   crow

TOMFOOLERY

Four Mile Creek
its bramblebush of dialects
They kept manhandling
Algonkian words—last century's Scottish miners—
& we all enjoy bunkum, flimflam,
moonshine
the jazz language North America

Up here's pettifog & taradiddle
(sleety rain fog cloud
spits down-ridge)
tomfoolery makes me think
of King Lear
I bet that's where it comes from
moor thrashed with night wind, lightning
(white quartz in blocks
on the far hill add
bedlam ghost hulks to storm)
Denver or DC this land of beguile, swindle, bilk, defraud
rock & each pine needle clump
sways its own careful pace
gypsy cant, bog Latin,
jackhammer sound in the distance, a truck
hauling Amazon boxes

 (night ponderosa shagged juniper really
snowing now
you can hear deer hooves
scrape the hillside

EXTINCT LANGUAGES
OF THE LEFT COAST

short list from Golla's book

Chimariko
Excelen
Wappo
Upper Coquille
Galice
Takelma
Waikuri
Coast Miwok
Plains Miwok
Nomlaki
Tubatulabal
Yahi
Sinkyone
Nongatl
Rumsen
Chalon
Mtusun Costonoan
Choynimni
Okwanuchu
New River Shasta
Obispeño Chumash
Konomihu
Rogue River Athabaskan
        &c.

WHEN I HEAR EMERALD TABLET

When I hear emerald tablet
    I think, Bolinas lagoon,
        & the question comes up,

    what pines stand on your coast points & ridges?

Bishop & Monterey
write my friends
        the dominant tree's Doug fir
    it marched down the slope

Redwood, coastal live oak, bay laurel stride through the watershed
or are trees
as in Algonkian, inanimate?

    Typesetting in June
when fog rolls in, the surface
    turns emerald, offshore wind scuffs it
        a white heron stands on one leg
        it's been there for centuries

    geōmantia, to read the grammar of earth

    'ilm al-raml, a science of sand

    Some say the art stems
from Hermes thrice greatest—
I wonder if coyote practiced it, or wild turkey
    from the beginning—
        we squint at Arcturas, orange star

high in the north
a slight red, *subrufa*, wrote Ptolemy

sky watcher

So we consider the seen and the unseen, O Hermes
the Miwok word for coyote, *kátwa-*

and Peter Warshall who studied the unseen metabolic pathways
took the long journey this month,
he left a science of soil,
now I hear *emerald*
          tablet I see him, working the drainage

west past Bolinas lagoon

P.W. in remembrance

GO LOOK UP IDEOLOGY

Go look up ideology
eye lands on dessertspoon
there's even a photo
of Harry Houdini
which makes me think of carnivals
cotton candy as a kid—
there it is, ideology, before flipping the page
        to peckish

DRIVING HOME FROM "KING LEAR"

Driving home from "King Lear"
county road under repair
four years ago floods tore it to pieces
        this year the West

is afire

Lear has gone the medicine path
burdock, nettle, hemlock, cuckoo flow'rs
in his hair

                    we all bite on something
madness or farther out
I like "rank fumiter" for its sound—
swept by a torrent, smoked flat
on a rock

Buddhists call it *duhkha*
someone always has it worse though
and the perigee-syzygy moon
yellow as
a sweet potato

sends out blessings of love

these vexéd
mountain peaks

IN A MOUNTAIN TOWN

In a mountain town
drinking coffee
someone's repairing a player piano in the
Western bar
taking the wall apart to get at felt-covered
hammers
Rough mountain town with assay office
A man says where do you live

"The next ridge south,
Sugarloaf"
"Haven't heard of it—"
shaking the tail of his coonskin

Then a caribou
clatters into town through the dream
one antler missing
other one carved with knobs
daubs of ceremonial ochre over white & black
designs.
Althea starts a dance
and I think of the night she was born
pink   wet   raising a howl as the
midwives placed her
in a tin grocery scale
"Where'd you get that dance?"

"From Mom before she
smelled bad
before she was dead."

ROBIN HOOD & THE BANKS

They lived by their hands, without any lands

Reading up on Scottish border ballads
in Bishop Percy's
     Reliques of Ancient English Poetry
his 19th c. editor notes the penalty
for taking one
of the king's deer—

    (all deer are the king's deer)
castration and your eyes
put out

Those well trained longbow fighters
              out of work,
land that once was commons now reserved for the Crown—
banding into a brother-and-sisterhood,
guerillas of the food chain
intimates of the watershed
           always eluding the sheriff.
Old time hackers, they cull
the privatized herds

The great theft of course
is *bucks*
          bucks of the Royal Family.
I would like our Thanksgiving
prayer drawn from
Robin Hood
maybe Walter Scott's rare old volumes

How the hills of the High
and Middle March shall echo
          the day
     the banks collapse.

DOG TANK SPRING

Not a light
between here and Blanding
Comb Ridge breaks the landscape
where a swarm of dreams enters
the wintry tent

      Freud's old treatise
a handbook for seeing
more symbols I can't read under sandstone cliffs
balance them with Teton Sioux
dream songs
      looked up in the library

How-to-do-it
excavating the strange things
out of slickrock
Dog Tank Spring
bear paw
      bear paw
crumbled droppings
whole juniper berries
in the mash

Here it goes again
one more treaty broken—
solitary older Navajo man
in a pickup
watches the sunset
wavering cliffs of the Bears Ears Buttes
      reddening behind him

Winter Solstice 2017

OLD PAL

Didn't think you'd
need that detective book again
but sorry I took it without
asking—
you in a methadone
        morphine sleep.

Coral snake
stack of $100 bills on the cover
red rock piñon-juniper background

      That's what got me
I'd just visited
Cedar Mesa
old woman listening, listening,
drawing long skirts together

             rain   never reaches the ground

the granaries, kivas, cliff villages—
prickly pear & now

you go shortly to land
of the dead.
Horned human figures white & red.
"Around the next bend," your parting words,
that's what I heard

      old pal

      for Dale Pendell

AND HAD THE THROATS OF BIRDS

"I'm glad this
shitty thing
didn't stretch out past
twilight

jesus christ

if we can
still help each other
and I think we can
let's"

Dale Pendell
1947-2018

THE DEATH OF BOBBIE LOUISE HAWKINS

Under the influence of
pratibhā,
      instinct, an old grammarian says

creatures act.
Only neotenic humans take so much training.

Who can change the towhee's song?
One weaves a nest,
one digs a lair, one finds the hidden seep
where a purple tufted
medicine flower roots.
Eat, love, fear
          fly, swim

the young of every species do.
These are facts
     of grammar.

Bobbie and I never got along too good.
Through the dark winter, from a
wall of night-soaked pines

     to-wit   to-wit   to-wit   to-wit

"The obscure bird clamor'd
     the live-long Night"

Some kind of owl?
No one I speak to seems to know.

May 2018

79

KṢEMENDRA'S CAUTION

Untrained the poet
gets tangled by his own thoughts.
The poem's a snarl.
Words scrape like brambles.
Speaking at a salon he can't find his way—
a clown
stranded downtown
right where the foreign streets
get weird.

Kavikaṇṭhābharaṇa 5.1

A SNAKE IN MATHURA

Miyan Shamsuddin Faridi
all his life disguised himself as an artist,
                someone on Youtube notes

he was a Sufi saint.
In Mathura playing Raga Puriya

        a black cobra came and coiled quietly
near.
Someone noticed
and the crowd killed it

Shamsuddin stopped playing, Why, he said,
why

        did you kill the snake?
He came to hear Puriya.

Miyan Shamsuddin Faridi Desai
spends his time
at the Dargahs of saints.
        "He believes

                in everlasting beauty."

SOMEHOW

Not sure how I go through
morning zazen with troubled groin joint
one aspect of suffering is lost trust & old friends
Turtle Old Man has been fashioning
beads grinding & piercing the little shells
on a KPFA reel-to-reel tape
since 1949
He asks the travelers to bring obsidian
but Coyote fell to earth the borrowed blackbird feathers
failed
These days Sulphur Bank
where he landed
stews with mercury from the abandoned mine,
a touch of the 20ᵗʰ century
yellow tailings invisible toxins
drizzle into Clear Lake for decades
I keep getting messages from Academia.com
to sell me scholarly papers about the contaminants—
(see Kroeber who says Oleyeme,
headwater of Putah Creek's
named for coyote "in all
the surrounding
        languages."

POISON METALS

"Śiva, when will I tear up the roots of my karma?"

Think about it different.
          Try something else.   What?
Another lawsuit details poisonous acts in the local Buddhist
group

          DANGER RADIOACTIVE

    who cleans up when the uranium mine
closes? who put up the fence?
          NO TRESPASSING

   molybdenum   tungsten   mercury   lead

a few ravens crisscross the
          evening sky

          bare feet
          blue throat
     rudrāksha prayer beads
a long string of bad moves disappearing into
          the past

THE BUSINESS OF BOOKS

The people's
republic of Berkeley
once had many collectives
(workers owned the business: no boss
but yourselves

"Bookpeople" in the eighties
we'd wheel carts up wide aisles
boxcutter in hand
to repack gay sunshine & fix your VW titles
handbooks to grow dope

Workers wore ponytails or eyeshadow
women & men
at the same tasks
a cook fixed grand lunches.
softball, rock 'n roll
          (maybe too much cocaine)

We all learnt to drive truck,
cartons heading up to Lavender Menace
in Toronto,
City Lights over the Bay

and published some too.
Dorn's *Gunslinger*
that slick initial *G* a lever-
action rifle part designed by anarcho-graphic
wizard
M. Myers,
At 5:00 p.m. you knock off and get beer.

Now picture those voiceless Amazon robots
whirring
up & down aisles to pack books
No long hair no drug-sweat no
softball no anarchist jokes
      What if no fun and no lunch—?

AFTER BHARTRIHARI

Don't try to change anyone's mind
Be quiet near animals
Figure out the torque of grammar, heft of words
In the assembly hall don't talk anyone down
not even the clownish
Know one or two shapes death takes
Watch the Great Bear drop through the sky
Go north and listen
        to the oldest of books

DELETE

In the once common world of PAPER documents
all sorts of
items got lost,
some tragic, some comic—

> flood
> mold
> wildfire
> chewed on by rats
> recycled inadvertently
> burrowing mice
> unexpected fits of rage
> constricting shame made you throw it all out
> coffee stains or wine spill
> disinterest
> infuriating misplacement
> white ants
> car crash
> eviction & your stuff impounded
> gas explosion at home or at work
> cat piss
> copy centers lost it
> puppy vomit
> broken water pipes

In the digital realm, Edward Snowden says
there is
no such thing as

> delete.

COLD MOUNTAIN

A windswept burn zone
high on a talus strewn mountain
snow, hail, and hard sun chase each other like
dogs.
Mountain bikes
rarely come up this high.
When they do they don't see what I see.
There's the occasional cougar
you can open a book by Ezra Pound—
otherwise no one
talks over the fine points
of poetry.

for Amelia Hall

OUT OF PARADISE

My former sister in law lived her whole
adult life in the California foothills town,
Paradise

      a trailer most of those years
ponderosa pine and Doug fir her neighbors
raised two boys
herself

Finally got a bungalow, paid it off,
retired

      then the flames

Today it's a cheap rental in Oroville
to the south
I called her Thanksgiving, she was eating at Denny's,
clothes, and her red jeep gone.
Talks of going back though—

what a tough lady, single mother, danced at my
wedding in a narrow aquamarine gown
drawing the eyes of all the men—
blonde hair free & long
Not to get burnt

      out of Paradise

GAME TRAIL

Animal trails wind through almost all wild landscapes. Meanwhile, about every road in North America that fits the lay of the land—that follows a river or valley, links woodland townships, heads into the hills, or winds up a mountain pass—was first laid down by big animals. Gridwork neighborhoods and long federal highways are the main exceptions.

That road that takes you to a lake or river? Deer, elk, moose, coyote, bear, or cougar took it first. They cut tracks through the brush and knew the best way through the hills; when "the bear went over the mountain," he probably took an established route. Trackers and hunters, then doctors, gamblers, traders, and people looking for lovers, walked along tracks laid down millennia earlier. Eventually came horses, carts, wagons. When the automobile arrived it too traveled "the old ways."

Ghost herds of fauna, our first civic planners. Let's call roads game trails for a while. It might be instructive to get a book on animal tracks. To study it is to see a world that lies beneath our own.

FORMS OF WRITING

The classic Chinese account
that writing starts with bird tracks in the sand
has its appeal

      Catullus, himself notably
indiscrete, says some things
should only get written
on water

        Did you hear there's
a natural history of type fonts
the Washington lever-action press
doth squeak
ephemera from a few high
quality print shops.

Firewood arrives from Granby,
all of it lodgepole, all of it beetle-kill.
Local pines
reclaim their ground where the Black
Tiger Fire once burnt

      Bark beetle heartwood bore,
inky squiggles, indigo curlicues,
inventive dingbats
&&&& in many hues
bacteria blues
Now cabinet makers covet the wood

We all leave traces where we've passed.
spindly tracks
ciphers inscribed about the post,
right where the bark's been scraped—
telling old escapades, romance,
now make a better story
        than most.

WATER AND FIRE

Struggling with the Sanskrit
of a poem
1400 years old,
keyaṃ tvarā means what?
Something like, why the big hurry.
So I go get coffee at the Blue Owl.
Banana bread's fresh this morning,
guy with a rough-trimmed beard tells me.
It's his mother's recipe.
A firefighter too—last month
got called with his truck out to Paradise.
The worst he's ever seen.
That's California but it sure could happen here.
We in this world living are water
the old poet says controlling her grief,
we trickle from the mouth
of a clay pot.
Fire, though, and I put a few dollars
in the tip jar,
that's something else.

ROHINI

I've been looking at the song
of Rohini, in the world's first
book of women's verse, the *Therigatha*.
What catches me is the open trusting talk with her father
She's young—Rohini can mean someone just
starting to menstruate

She lived 2500 years ago
a thronging city on the wide alluvial plain formed by the Ganges
buffalo, cattle, horse, wagon, camel caravans
press through

      Well, what excites Rohini are the saffron robe
seekers who walk past her home
requesting food in little bowls
Young, they live without money or houses
sleep in woods between towns
Dirty & wild—to her they look sober,
act generous
She begs her father to let her
join the adventure

      and calls them *samana,*
a Pali word. Scholars think it might be
where the Tungus people
got their term *shaman*

I like Rohini's idealism, the urge to get going
knew women much like her once
                              (where did they go?
The *samana* own little, just rag-patch robes
They don't lay a trip on Rohini for being
middleclass though
She likes that they love each other
hailing from far-off districts they
don't hold their parents' crabbed disregard
for outsiders

She's telling her father she needs
to go with them
He seems a good sort—baffled but listens close—
finally gets what makes her ardent.
                              We know from
the poem he let her go, his teenage daughter

Thanks to her life looks bigger
Filling clay jugs with money
stuffing them under the floor makes
scant sense
        No way to tell if he went on the road too
the poem won't say.

Ox-cart extensive dust tracks North India
constellations "deer head" and "archer" crackle portentously

95

a northern horizon the jagged blue crest of
      Himalaya

O Rohini
bare feet, patch robe, tough discipline
vivid these years your poem.

A MILAREPA SHRINE IN LADAKH

Squat stone monk quarters up in the clouds.
Headwaters of the Indus. The icy mist comes in shreds, then
a quick windblown glimpse: red boulders, white tundra
grass, a toothy rock overhang. The valley's known for blue
sheep since elderly lamas keep hunters away. But the spring-
fed pool iced up a month ago, the sheep drifted down-valley
for water. Jackrabbits—the *ribong* with coarse fur that's truly
blue—leap between rocks. And chakora birds flap upwards
to vanish into the hillside. All make a living off stubbly
orange tundra plants.

On a sloped rim of granite, the whitewall shrine
has a hand-painted board, "Elevation 14,400 Feet." That's
the same as Mount Rainier or Mount Shasta! Inside, a bare
bulb, two winking butter lamps. A larger than life gold-
plated Milarepa flanked by bronze figures I don't recognize
looks bemused. He's the poet from the Trans-Himalaya
plateau everyone back home knows. *Can blue sheep reach
enlightenment?* Two older lamas in smoke-engulfed robes
confer. Their eyes glitter by the blackened tea churn.

"Next time you come, stay two weeks."

The lama blessed my prayer beads
in front of Milarepa
it's the māla you gave me
four lapis lazuli beads for counting
two tiny bone skulls on the hemp cord

Remember these mountains
walking them together

many drainages east but cold jags of mist the same
I admire your good-humored pluck

mornings we swapped dreams

ate watery potato soup for
two whole weeks
back & forth across the milky glacial runoff creeks
scary ice-crusted logs under our boots

Thirty-three years ago and you're dead now
Sharing jokes
halfway up the world's
high slopes

Kristina Loften 1952-2015

IDEOGRAM ONLY TO GUESS AT

How can I sit in the sun & snow
reading you, Ezra Pound?
Younger poets
find your mistakes unatonable—
the rants against Jews
support for Mussolini's steel fists,
those incomprehensible Greek sentences
Chinese pictographs
even the late Egyptian hieroglyphs
that make your pages arcane.
Did you have a heart of love hidden away?
I would stop reading
but Ezra, there is unexplained karma
            between us.

"And as to why they go wrong,
thinking of rightness"—
your words old man,
at the end something deeper than madness?
Did you imprisoned for treason
or was it insanity
in a ward upstairs,
Saint Elizabeth's Hospital,
know that below in obstetrics
I'd come into the world?
That's what my Socialist Jewish mother told me.
karma is dark, hard to read as a poem,
            ideogram only to guess at.

Our nation today
has for leaders a band of thugs
you would find loathsome, as the young
poets I meet find you loathsome.
There is karma between us,
Ezra Pound.
Upstairs typing *Rock Drill* while the nation
arms itself for new war,
me downstairs puking & mewling—
the liberated poetry wards
        a nation crazy as you are.

HANAMATSURI

It's Buddha's birthday in a spare
four mat pine &
stucco teahouse floored with straw.
Six of us back on haunches
ceremonially admire & slurp
the bright grassy *matcha* whipped in a handmade bowl.
Some utensils take poetic names
this day only.
Nobody knows the bamboo scoop's
real name but it gets a single-day epithet,
words from some dead poet.
Ironclad clouds above the rust-colored mountains.
Why do I hear Cleopatra's rebuke?
the stinging brass retort of a .30-30
cracking the higher peaks, the human heart?
"Though age from folly could not give me freedom,
It does from childishness."
Seems that I read too many books this winter.
Let's call the lever-action rifle
Woke Up Bear
even just for today,
blue growling clouds of the Indian Peaks,
first pang of ursine hunger on springtime claws
across the road and up the pine-filled draw.
As always, the tough blossom out early
is the smoke purple
pasque flower.
Welcome the baby Buddha!

14 April 2019

101

RIDDLERS, ROGUES, & CHILDREN

For several days
I've been reading about secret
languages
the author calls them dark tongues

Speakers hide mysteries inside what they speak

There's a break in the storm so I set
off for the mailbox
Two neighbor girls
bounce down on bicycles

"This is larkspur" says one, ditching her wheels,
"silver lupine...
kinnikinnik"
        she swipes her hand at the leaves

"And her name is Etteloc!" laughs the other—

In law or the English Department we call it jargon
Vulgate or cant
when swapped on the street
in England someone called it bog Latin

Etteloc, of course! the name
        spoken backwards, same thing as dog—
Colette returns to her bike.
In England at crossroads people heard ghost words,
they called it
        peddler's French

But children do it better than rogues,
riddlers, vagabonds
priests

So, Eihpos for you, let's look at that
green leaf again,
its name a fiddler's trick.
Forward is backwards, there's a bear in the berry
He'll set you a riddle:
      kinnikinnik.

WHERE THEY WENT

Raquel's flight to Venezuela was canceled
Today Aleisha leaves for Oakland if the planes fly
Morgan drove to her parents in Lincoln, Nebraska
Kiara is quarantined in Aurora with family members who
    are high risk
With his chosen family of eleven Kyle high risk has isolated
    in Colorado Springs
Cryptic as Mona Lisa, Allison says her sister made it out of
    New York
Andy with green hair upbeat helpful his eye a sparkle of pleasure
Dark in the screen Airesa keeps working at the grocery
Shreeya says the family situation in Kathmandu is worrisome
Essential worker at the BMW shop Sarah couldn't join us
Heading for Maryland Sam got placed in a patrol car
Last flight out Mayra made Bogotá now locked down two
    weeks at her mother's
Kendra lost all three jobs
Aradhika made it to Ashland
Andrew disinfects classrooms then locks them
A roommate of Alena's friend died of it
Anna lost her grandmother to the virus in New York

2 April 2020

AFTER THE CRICKET

Back east the New England landscapes
feel archaic, compressed
a friend's recent letter speaks of Mt. Greylock
Was it Herman Melville gave it the name?
Mound of blue conifer looks in my memory smoky
I spent a week
camped at its base

Little waterproof tent
my wife Kristina, Oliver who I worked with for years,
our midsize shepherd dog muddy prints on the swamp-colored
Army Surplus sleeping bags
We sorted books
         in a soft meadow all day

Someone near Pittsfield
had filled a barn with crazy old titles, lots on the
architecture of early cathedrals—now wanted
to sell 'em.
200 cartons we packed & shipped West
to the collectivist bookshop
we worked at.

Finally in my 67th year
I'm figuring out that jagged, jumbled up
cracked granite snarl of the Indian Peaks
carved into pitching shapes during the last ice age.
the drainages are called Blue, Green,
Rainbow, Jasper,
and there's blocky old Devil's Thumb

elk going over the passes longer than all human history
hoof tracks mark the scary snow cornices

Chasms, chessmen, pinnacles, chutes
lurching spires we call hoodoos,
relict glaciers & ice-fed lakes
that clench your balls up into your belly
It's *Tao te Ching*
and *Farmer's Almanac* crunched by three
billion years into one granite treatise
a text no one could figure out
          in one lifetime.

In the foothills crickets arrived overnight—
Julia Seko once told me
the elderly gardeners of Longmont
who work the unforgiving soil beneath Long's Peak
say snow comes six weeks
after
the cricket.

THE FACTS AT DOG TANK SPRING

Three broke-down gnarled cottonwoods at Dog Tank Spring
they're older than anything at Dog Tank Spring
The cloudy iced water the high desert
two or three inches fresh rabbit track snow
Blaze orange and cobalt tents at Dog Tank Spring
The crackling juniper fire at Dog Tank Spring
The night stars wheeling close and mythically overhead
you could reach up & touch the sharp edges of
constellations at Dog Tank Spring
Half human petroglyphs haunt the dream at Dog Tank Spring
but who talks about Aeschylus at Dog Tank?
Orange sparks sift into the night
a coyote cries off in the sage at Dog Tank
Wonder where the dead go at Dog Tank Spring
Dog Tank Spring turkey buzzards go where?
Dog Tank hiking comrades shout over wine at the night sky
At Dog Tank Spring your cell phone don't work
the news went stale a thousand years past
night drops to 12 degrees
the water jug freezes at Dog Tank Spring
Plans hopes aspirations irresistible ideas at Dog Tank Spring
but human designs at daybreak seem the raving of idiots
dawn is for coffee at Dog Tank Spring
At Dog Tank Spring the bow saw the axe the work gloves the matches
the Cedar Mesa map at Dog Tank Spring
spires hoodoos pinnacles of polished red sandstone
cream colored stone shelves at Dog Tank Spring
The trail guide says anticline & upwarp at Dog Tank Spring
Greasewood rattlesnake blue wavering laccoliths
the tiny oil painting tacked to a pinyon

by someone last month at Dog Tank Spring
A hundred years are what at Dog Tank Spring
Dog Tank past and future lead nowhere
What are spilloffs chockstones scorpions the dugway the sidereal
what's a rowel at Dog Tank Spring?
The faraway ranch-house the constellations the rabbitbrush
the anvil-headed clouds over Navajo
Let's talk about the old ones at Dog Tank Spring
Tobacco Canyon Bullet Canyon Kane Gulch the turkey pen ruins
want to meet here in late March?
Embers whiten and fade they're fleeting books or old loves
a wool blanket over the cold sleeping bag.
These things are facts
at Dog Tank Spring.

18-20 December 2019
for Mike Golston

FOXES

Of the world's foxes
I learnt most
from that female harassed a
coyote   barking her bright
scrap of a yap
down the grass ridge
following who had taken her
crumpled foil treasure
a charred potato.
Then there's Pai Chang's fox—
Old man,
do not forget
cause & effect.

NOTES

Tenth Song of the Meadowlark: Begun on the same track as *From the Arapaho Songbook* and *A Possible Bag*, where untitled stanzas link together through repeated words, echoed lines, and recurrent themes. But the new poems quietly revolted, asserting separate identities, asking for titles. They continue the sequence in a different mode.

"A Cheremiss Song." Cheremiss are a Finnish people of Eastern Russia. Anselm Hollo, Finnish born American poet.

"Mount Blanca with Ute Creek at Dawn." Written for an event at the Denver Art Museum. The title comes from a landscape by Stephen Hannock, directly in the monumental style of Thomas Moran and Albert Bierstadt. But look close: postmodern twists start to emerge peopling the ecology with pop culture stencils. A three-panel screen by Maynard Dixon, elsewhere in the museum's Western Art collection, added a few ideas.

"Wolf Acrostic." Young's book: *The Wolves of North America*, 1944.

"Arapaho Ghost Dance Songs." Recorded by James Mooney, Irish-American Land League activist, ethnographer, advocate for the peyote ritual: *The Ghost-Dance Religion and the Sioux Outbreak of 1890*. Of ghost dance songs, Mooney considers the Arapaho "first in importance, for number, richness of reference, beauty of sentiment, and rhythm of language." A bare-bone lyric here: visions turned into music. *Heiso-noonin*, our father, refers to Wovoka (Jack Wilson the Paiute prophet). Thanks to Andrew Cowell, Alonzo Moss, Sr., and William J. C'hair for modern orthography: *Arapaho Stories, Songs, and Prayers*. Also Cowell and Moss, *Arapaho Grammar*.

"Trees of the John Muir Way." Project designed by Alec Finlay of Edinburgh for the centennial of Muir's death in 2014. Four of us planted twenty-five seedlings as a botanical poem, between Muir's birthplace Dunbar in the east, and Helensburgh in the west where the nine-year-old Muir left for America. A walk of 130 miles.

"And Had the Throats of Birds." Dale Pendell: poet, plant lore & science, counterculture historian. W. B. Yeats, "Cuchulain Comforted."

"Water and Fire." The old poem: *Subhāṣitāvalī*, no. 1059. I have not published a translation. A version by W.S. Merwin and J.M. Masson appears in *The Peacock's Egg*.

"Rohini." See Andrew Schelling and Anne Waldman, *Songs of the Sons and Daughters of Buddha* (2020), for Rohini's song. For a translation with original Pali, Charles Hallisey, *Therigatha: Poems of the First Buddhist Women*.

"Riddlers, Rogues, & Children." Susan Howe, *Debths*; Daniel Heller-Roazen, *Dark Tongues*.

"After the Cricket." Audrey DeLella Benedict, *The Southern Rockies*.

"Foxes." *Mumonkan*, case 2.

ABOUT THE AUTHOR

ANDREW SCHELLING, poet and translator. Author of twenty-odd books including *From the Arapaho Songbook* and *The Real People of Wind & Rain.* In the 1970s studied classics with Norman O. Brown and ecology of mind with Gregory Bateson at U.C. Santa Cruz, then up to Berkeley for Sanskrit while editing samizdat poetry journals. In 1990 he moved over the Continental Divide to the Front Range of the Southern Rockies with wife and daughter. Has worked on land use, wolf reintroduction, defiance to dams, protection of wilderness. Eight books of poetry translated from Sanskrit & related tongues. His study *Tracks Along the Left Coast: Jaime de Angulo & Pacific Coast Culture* is a folkloric account of bohemian poets, old time West Coast storytelling, natural history, cattle rustling, & linguistics. Many years teaching poetry and Sanskrit at Naropa University, he lives in the mountains west of Boulder, Colorado.